EAT MY Glitter DUST

ILLUSTRATED BY LUCY KIRK

EAT MY Glitter DUST

POSITIVE WORDS FOR SELF-CARE

LOM
ART

First published in Great Britain in 2020 by LOM ART,
an imprint of Michael O'Mara Books Limited
9 Lion Yard
Tremadoc Road
London SW4 7NQ

A CIP catalogue record for this book is available from the British Library.

Papers used by Michael O'Mara Books Limited are natural,
recyclable products made from wood grown in sustainable
forests. The manufacturing processes conform to the
environmental regulations of the country of origin.

ISBN: 978-1-912785-34-6 in hardback print format
ISBN: 978-1-912785-35-3 in ebook format

1 2 3 4 5 6 7 8 9 10

Designed by Natasha LeCoultre

Printed and bound in China

www.mombooks.com

MIX
Paper from
responsible sources
FSC® C016973

FSC
www.fsc.org

*Disclaimer: No unicorns were
injured in the making of this book.

INTRODUCTION

When you've had a bad day, have you ever wished there was someone who could tell you what to do? This little book is packed with motivating quotes and life advice covering topics including love, friendship, work, and everything else in-between, from your very own fairy godmother unicorn.

Eat My Glitter Dust will remind you to be fabulous in every aspect of your life, to work hard but play harder, be your best authentic self, celebrate the sweet things in life (coffee, doughnuts, friends), and spend time with nature . . . even if the most adventurous you usually get is watering the three succulents on your windowsill.

EAT

ICE CREAM

FOR

breakfast

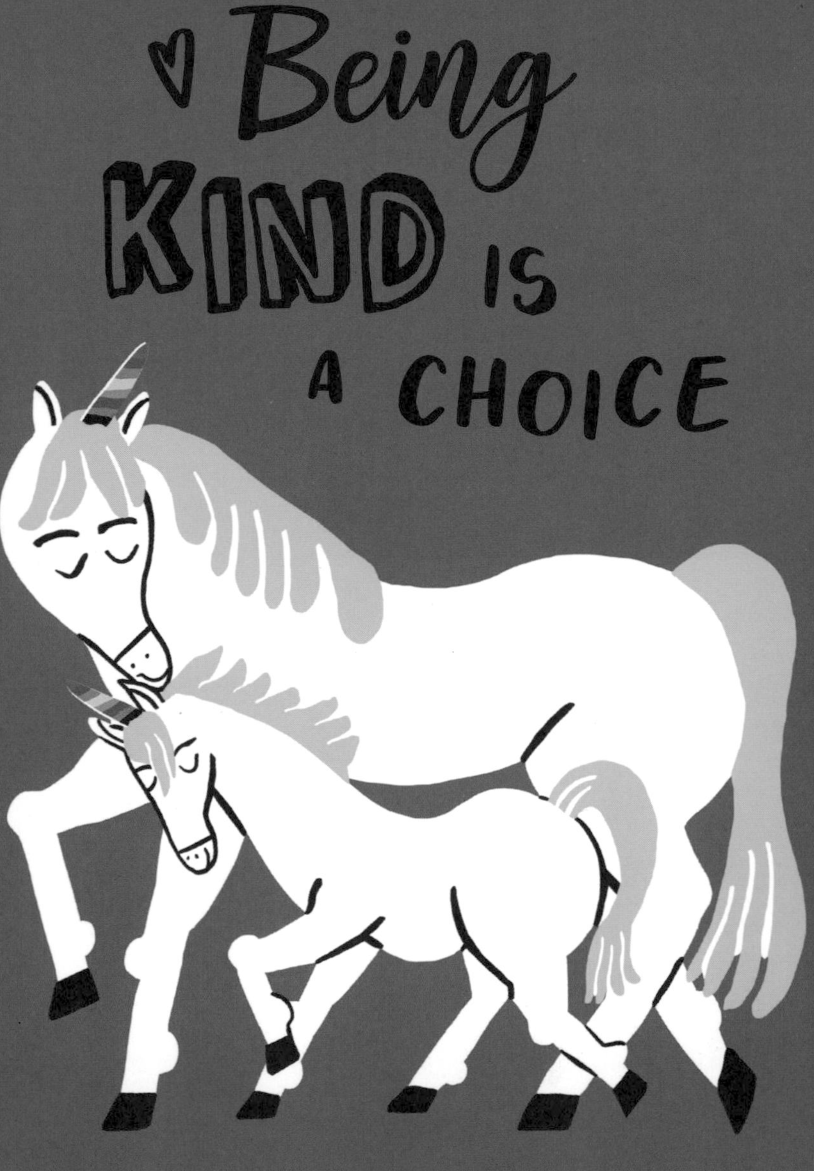
Being
KIND IS
A CHOICE

PLANT

BASED

LIFE

BE YOUR BEST *extra self*

MAKE EVERYTHING

sparkle

Life IS WHAT HAPPENS WHEN YOU'RE LOOKING AT YOUR PHONE

IT'S OK
TO BE PRICKLY
SOMETIMES

March FOR YOUR FUTURE

UNLEASH
YOUR
diva

Brunch
LIKE NO ONE IS
WATCHING

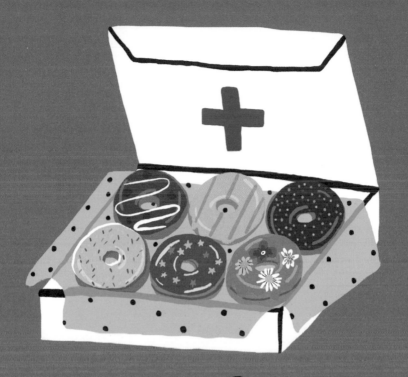

Doughnuts
F I X
EVERYTHING

BE Fierce

EVERY DAY

HAVING HIGH STANDARDS IS SELF CARE

Love
YOURSELF
FIRST

TAKE A COMPLIMENT

Love
is
LOVE

Chocolate
UNDERSTANDS
HEART-
BREAK

LOVE IS COLOURFUL AND messy

IT'S NOT OVER
UNTIL YOU
UNFRIEND

EVERYONE
DESERVES
TO BE TREATED
LIKE A
queen

WORK
HARD,
chill
HARDER

FRIENDS

ARE FREE

therapy

Best friends
ARE FOR LIFE

(BECAUSE THEY KNOW TOO MUCH)

GOOD FRIENDS
DON'T LET YOU DO STUPID THINGS
...alone

YOUR *squad*
IS ALL YOU
NEED

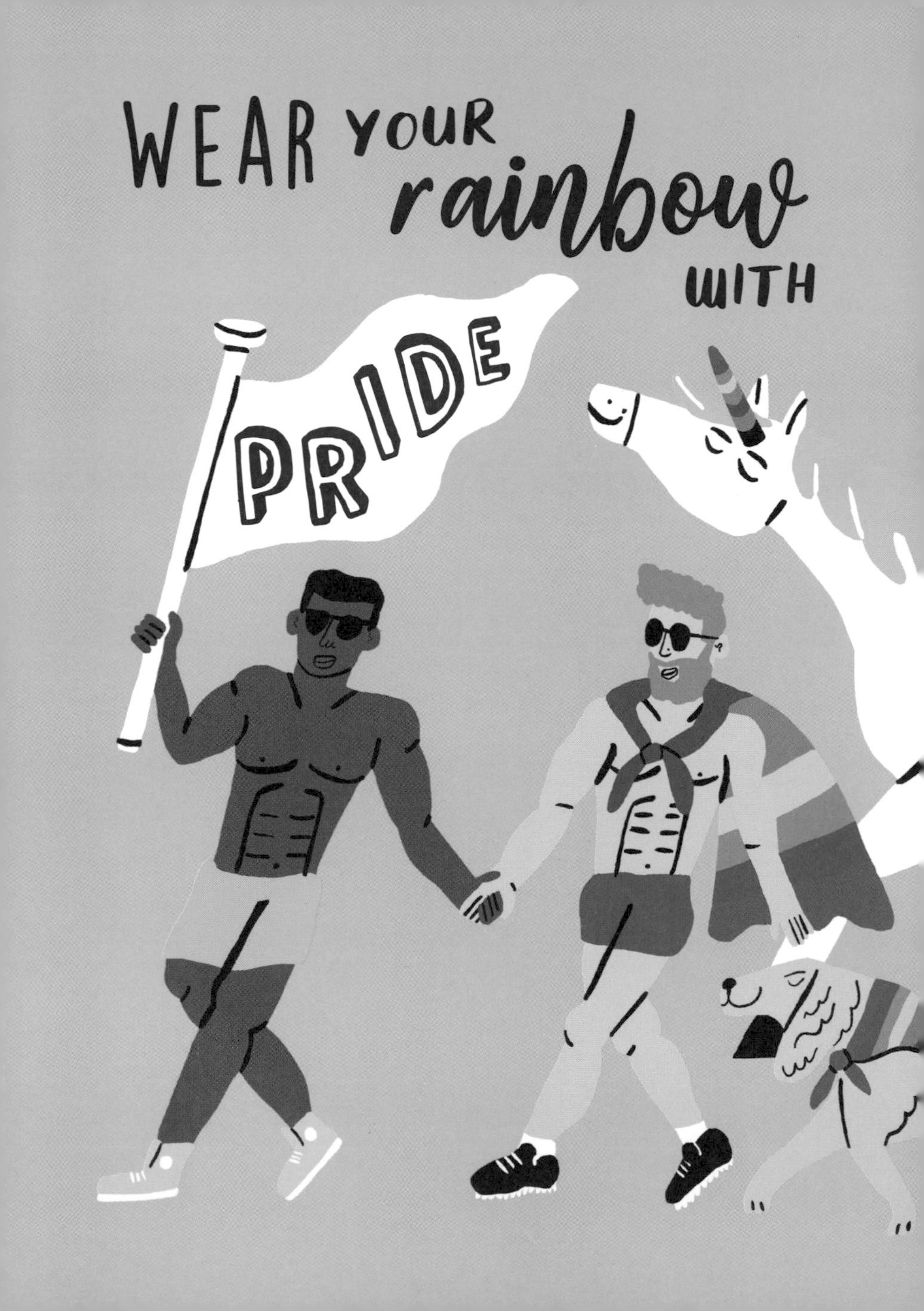
WEAR YOUR rainbow WITH
PRIDE

Indulge AT ALL TIMES

FRIENDS WHO
∞ slay TOGETHER,
∞ stay ∞
TOGETHER

EMBRACE *difference*

SAY
NO
TO
TOXIC
PEEPS

DRESS
LIKE
EVERYONE IS
WATCHING

CLOSE **DEALS** IN *heels*

EVERYTHING
IS YOURS
FOR THE
TAKING
HUNNY

IF AT FIRST YOU DON'T SUCCEED, TRY IT AGAIN *with glitter*

DON'T BE
Sorry

Mirror, mirror
ON THE *wall...*
GET UP AGAIN
IF YOU **FALL**

HUMP DAYS
ARE *play*
days

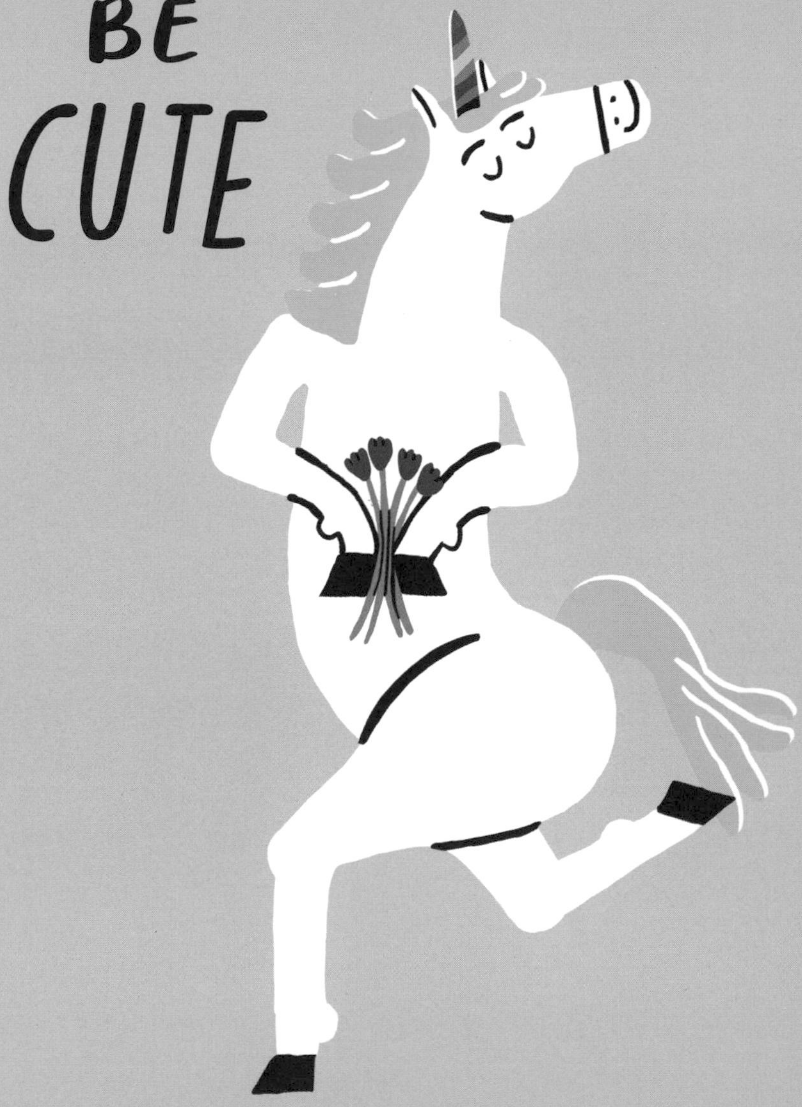
BE
CUTE

ALWAYS BE READY

TO GO **OUT** OUT...

SPRAY, DELAY AND walk away

TREAT YO'SELF

THE BRIGHTER

THE BETTER

RETROGRADE-
STAY INSIDE

Please

DO
NOT
DISTURB

MOISTURIZE,
MOISTURIZE,
MOISTURIZE

CONFIDENCE

IS

EVERYTHING

ZEN OUT IN nature ONCE IN A WHILE

SUNDAYS ...

NAMA'STAY
IN BED

ABOUT THE ILLUSTRATOR

Lucy Kirk is an illustrator and ceramist. She graduated from Brighton University in 2012, she has since worked on a wide range of projects. Her clients include Alexander McQueen, Kiehl's, Oprah's Bookclub, MAC, Refinery29, TRESemmé, Grindr, Camden Brewery, Jamie Cullum, Lush, Coal Yard Drops and Facebook.

W lucy-kirk.co.uk   @lucykirk